Tarik O'Regan

THE ECSTASIES ABOVE

Vocal score

NOVELLO

The Ecstasies Above

The Ecstasies Above, commissioned from the Robert Baker Commissioning Fund for Sacred Music by Yale Institute of Sacred Music, was premièred by Yale Schola Cantorum under the direction of Simon Carrington on 4 March 2007 in Woolsey Hall, Yale University.

The minimum number of singers required is 16 (two each per chorus part, together with the solo voices); however, a larger number for the main chorus (16-32 voices, for example) is more suitable. The string quartet and the two solo vocal quartets should be placed in front of the chorus. The vocal quartets should be spatially separated from each other. Depending on the venue and the size of the chorus, the string quartet may need to be amplified.

Tarik O'Regan
New York, August 2006

Text

ISRAFEL (Edgar Allan Poe)
In Heaven a spirit doth dwell
"Whose heart-strings are a lute";
None sing so wildly well
As the angel Israfel,
And the giddy stars (so legends tell),
Ceasing their hymns, attend the spell
Of his voice, all mute.

Tottering above
In her highest noon,
The enamoured moon
Blushes with love,
While, to listen, the red levin
(With the rapid Pleiads, even,
Which were seven),
Pauses in Heaven.

And they say (the starry choir
And the other listening things)
That Israfeli's fire
Is owing to that lyre
By which he sits and sings –
The trembling living wire
Of those unusual strings.

But the skies that angel trod,
Where deep thoughts are a duty –
Where Love's a grown-up God –
Where the Houri glances are
Imbued with all the beauty
Which we worship in a star.

[Therefore thou art not wrong,
Israfeli, who despisest
An unimpassioned song;
To thee the laurels belong,
Best bard, because the wisest!
Merrily live, and long!] *

The ecstasies above
With thy burning measures suit –
Thy grief, thy joy, thy hate, thy love,
With the fervour of thy lute –
Well may the stars be mute!

Yes, Heaven is thine; but this
Is a world of sweets and sours;
Our flowers are merely – flowers,
And the shadow of thy perfect bliss
Is the sunshine of ours.

If I could dwell
Where Israfel
Hath dwelt, and he where I,
He might not sing so wildly well
A mortal melody,
While a bolder note than this might swell
From my lyre within the sky.

* Stanza omitted

Duration: c. 18'

Instrumentation:
Chorus (SATB)
Eight soloists (SSAATTBB)
String quartet or string orchestra

Commissioned from the Robert Baker Commissioning Fund for Sacred Music
by Yale Institute of Sacred Music for Yale Schola Cantorum, Simon Carrington, Conductor

THE ECSTASIES ABOVE

Edgar Allan Poe
(1809 - 1849)

Tarik O'Regan
(b. 1978)

© 2009 Novello and Company Limited

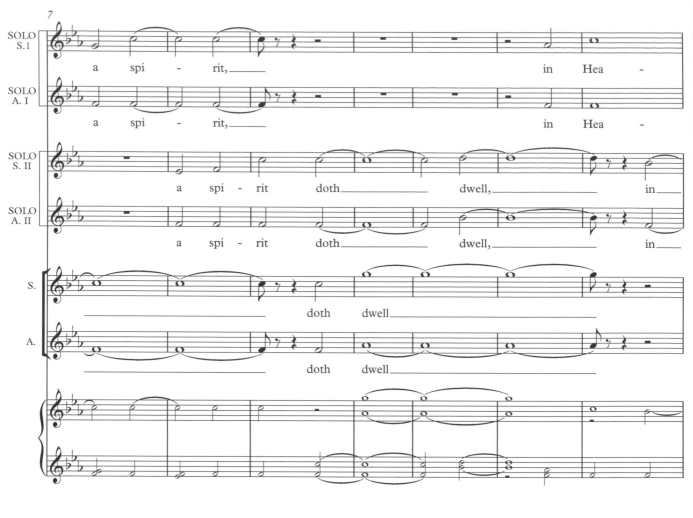

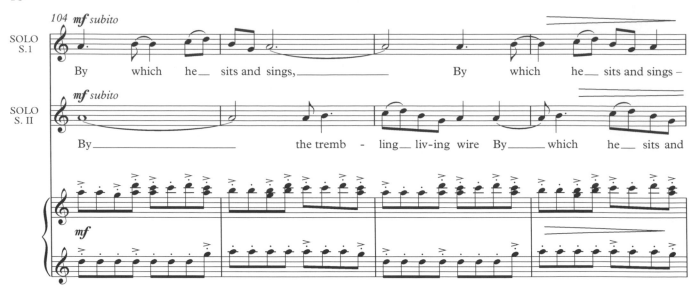

By which he sits and sings, By which he sits and sings –

By the tremb - ling liv-ing wire By which he sits and

The tremb - ling liv-ing wire Of those un - u-sual strings, Of those un - u-sual strings, Of those

sings – The tremb - ling liv-ing wire Of those un - u-sual strings, Of those un - u-sual strings,

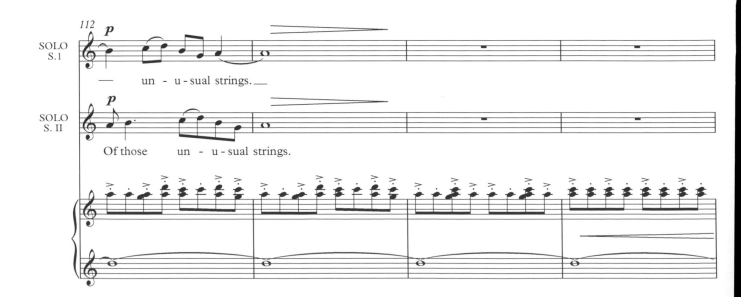

— un - u-sual strings. —

Of those un - u-sual strings.

Where the Hou-ri glan-ces are_____ Im-bued with all the beau-ty_____

Where the Hou-ri glan-ces are_____ Im-bued with all the beau-ty_____

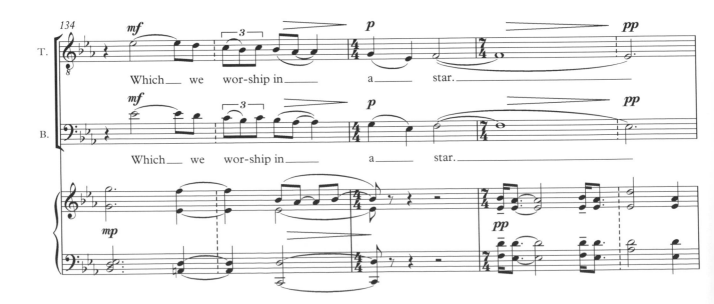

Which___ we wor-ship in_____ a_____ star._____

Which___ we wor-ship in_____ a_____ star._____

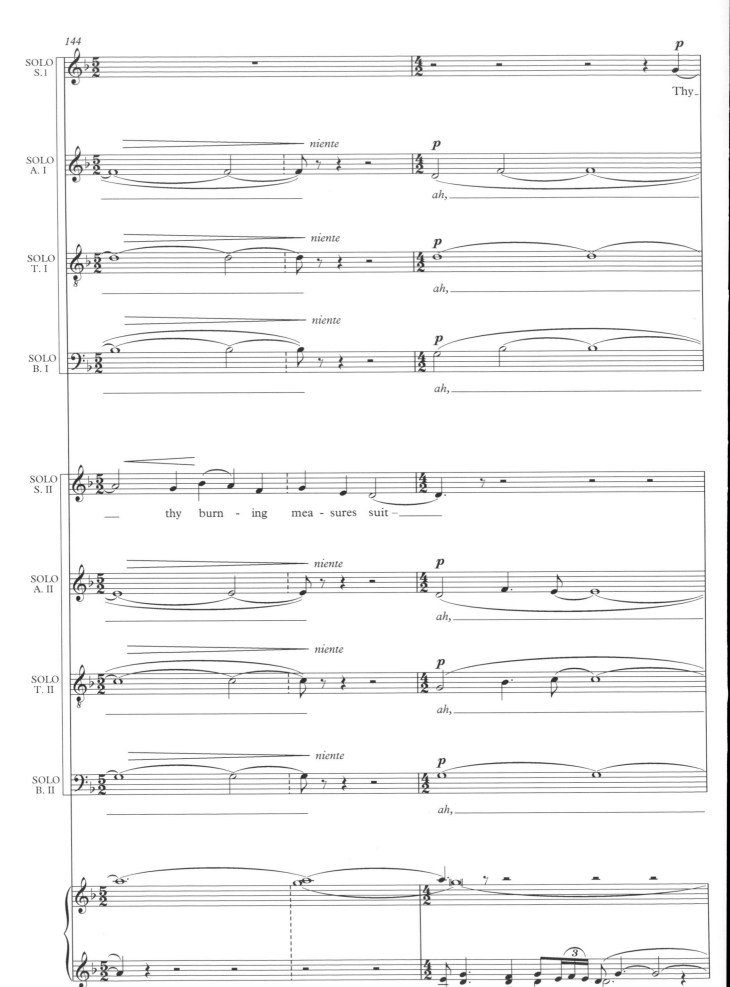

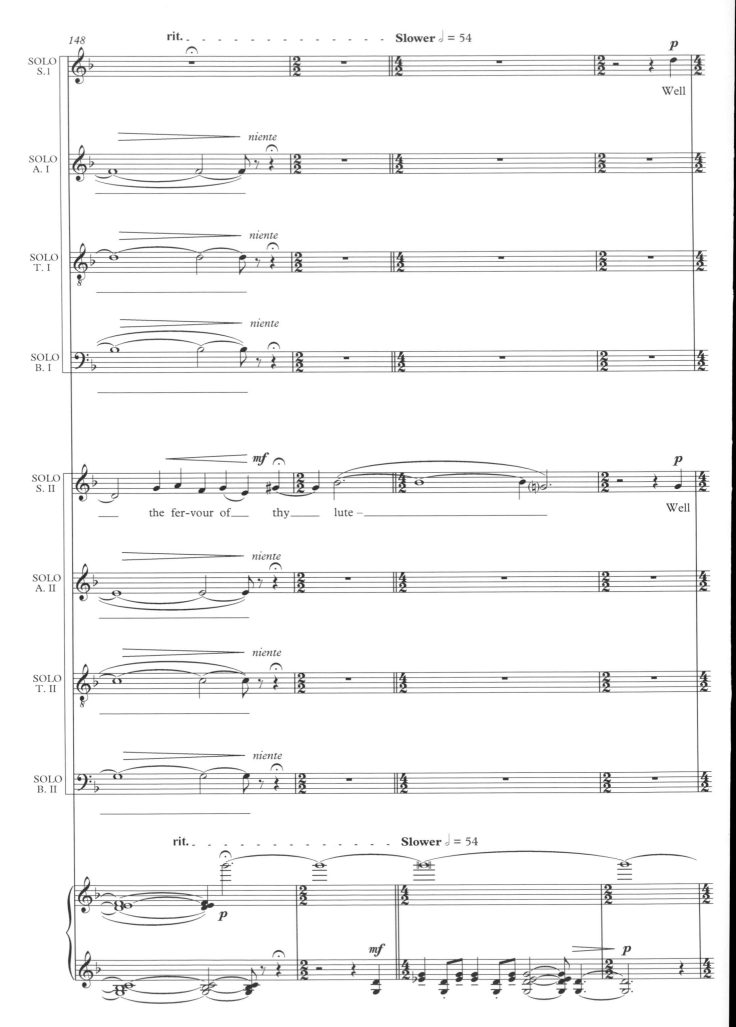

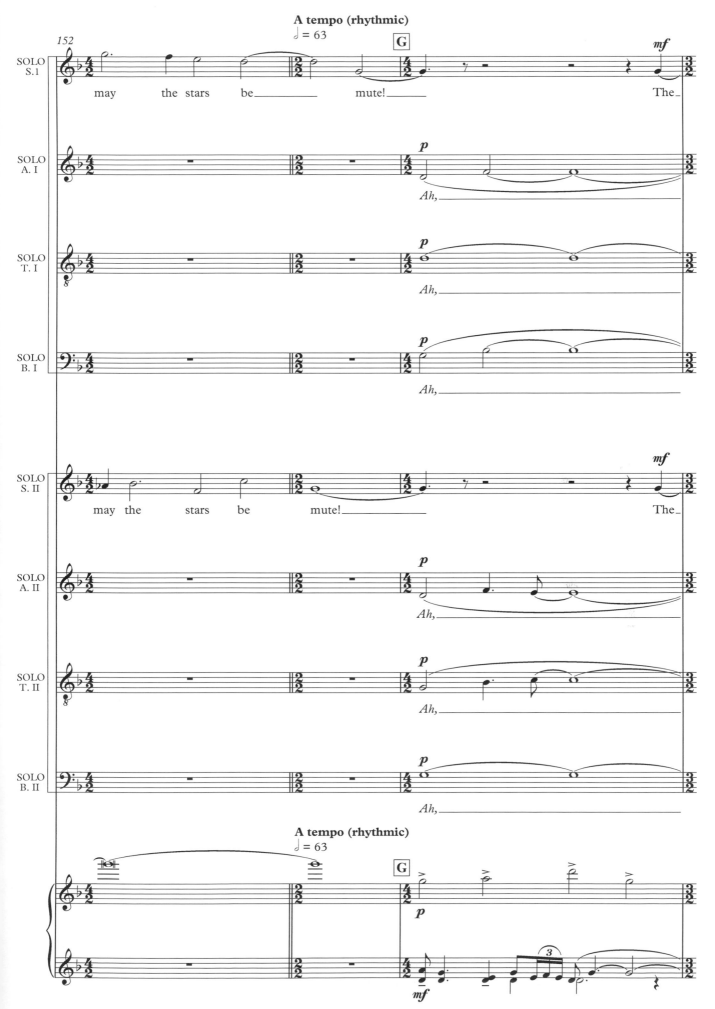

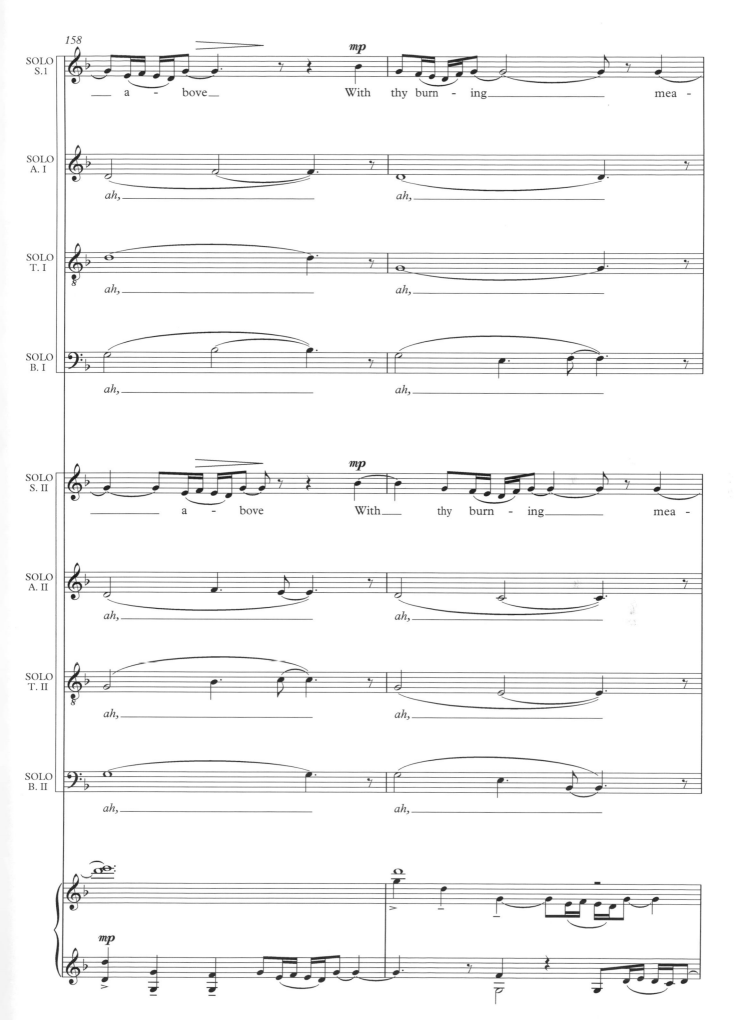

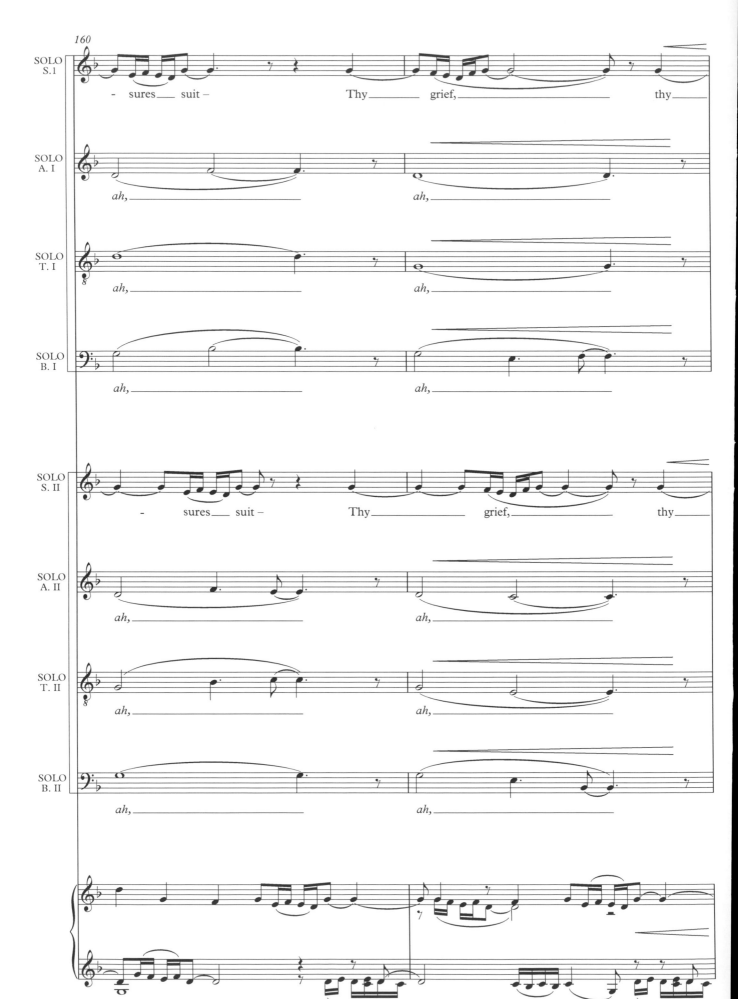

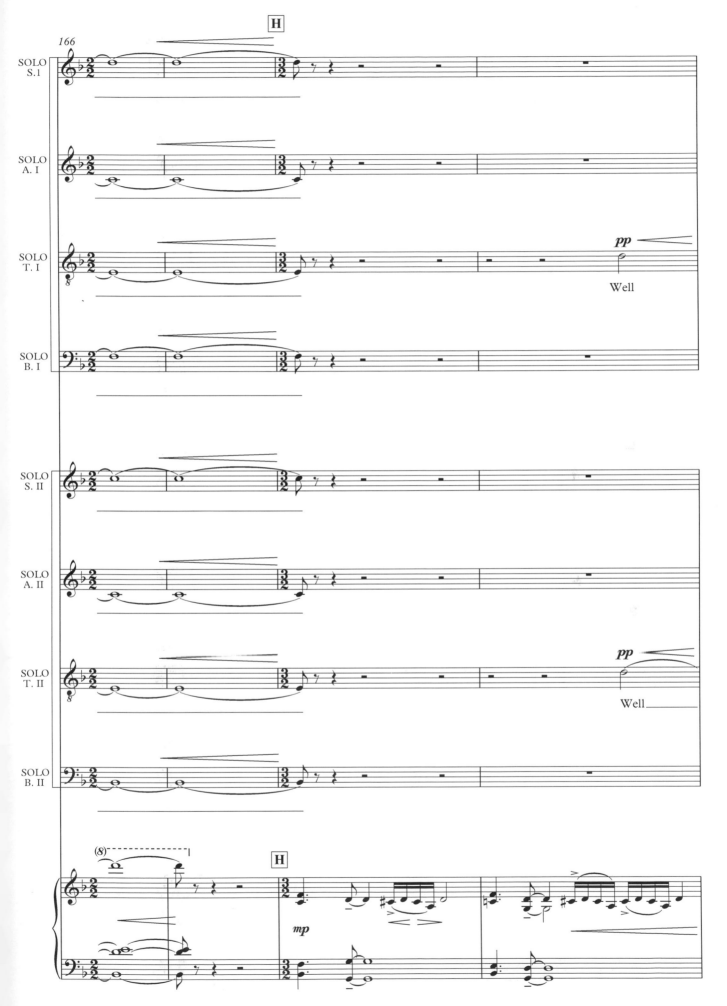

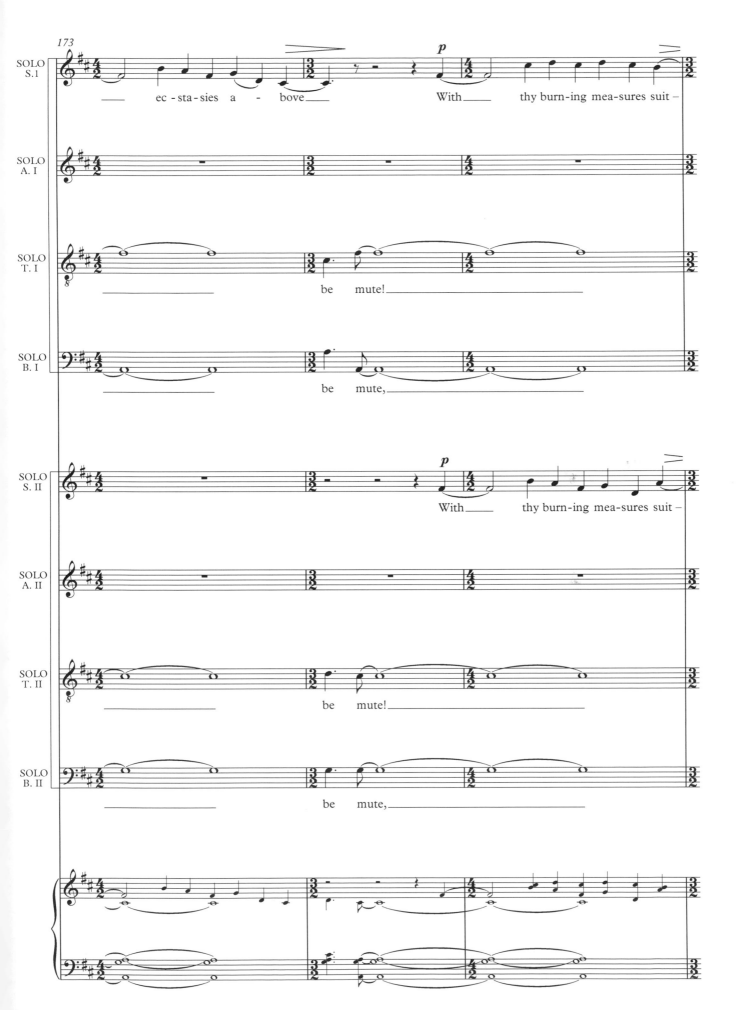

(strings play semiquavers here)

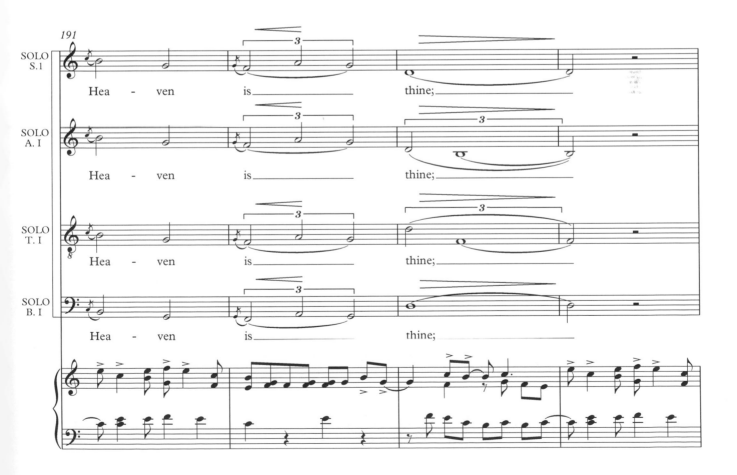

but_____ this Is a world of sweets and

but_____ this Is a world of sweets and

but_____ this Is a world of sweets and

but_____ this Is a world of sweets and

sours; Our flo - wers are mere - ly - flow -

sours; Our flo - wers are mere - ly - flow -

sours; Our flo - wers are mere - ly - flow -

sours; Our flo - wers are mere - ly - flow -

grief, thy joy, thy hate, thy love,

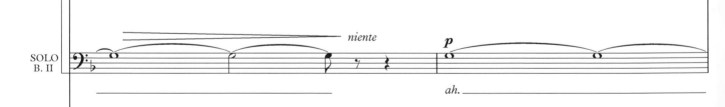

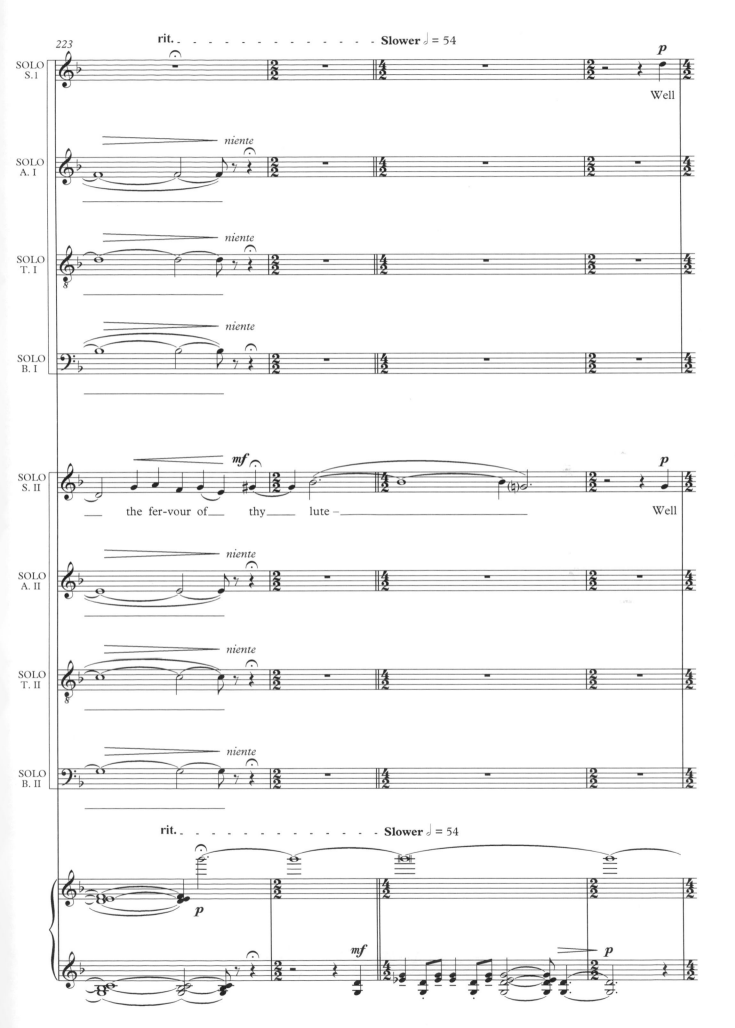

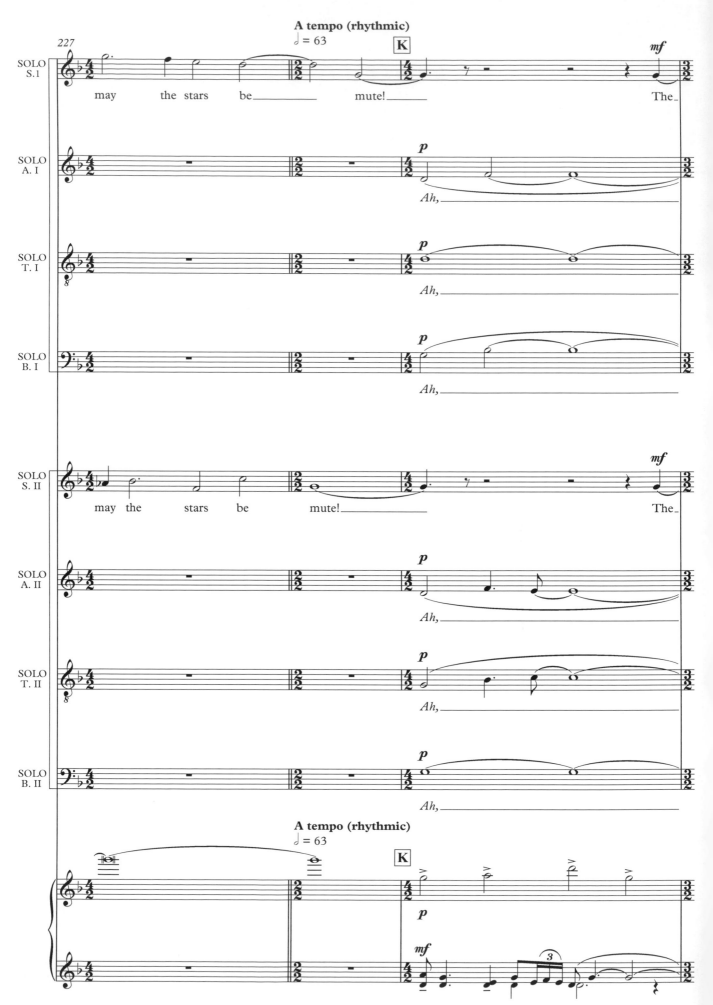

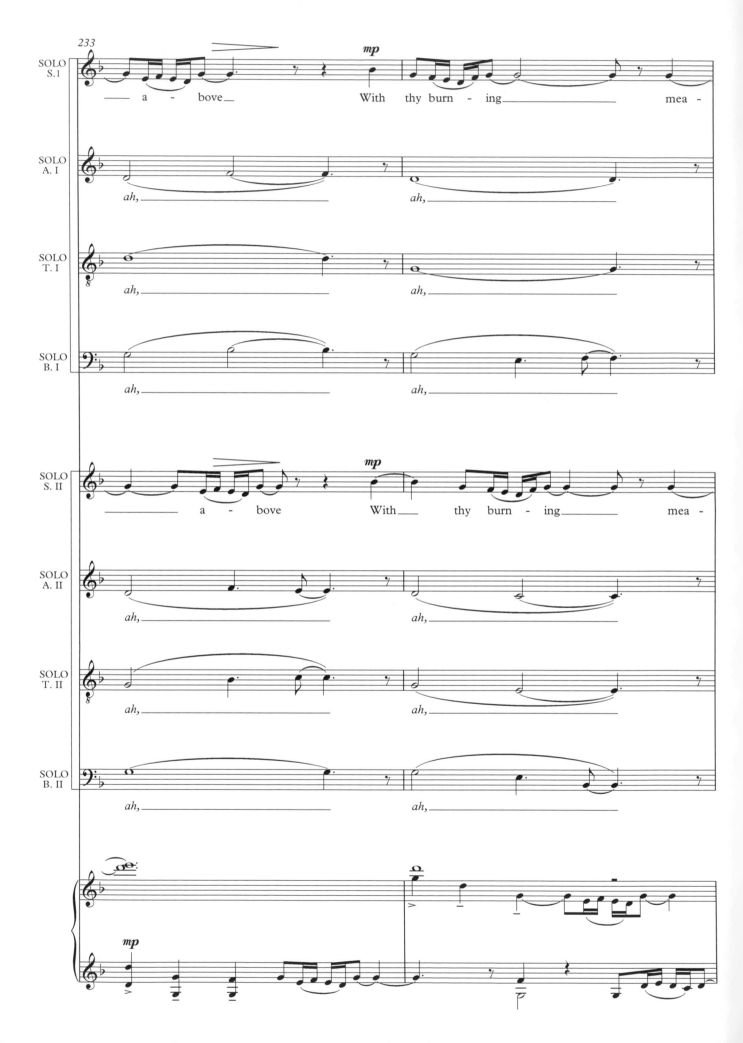

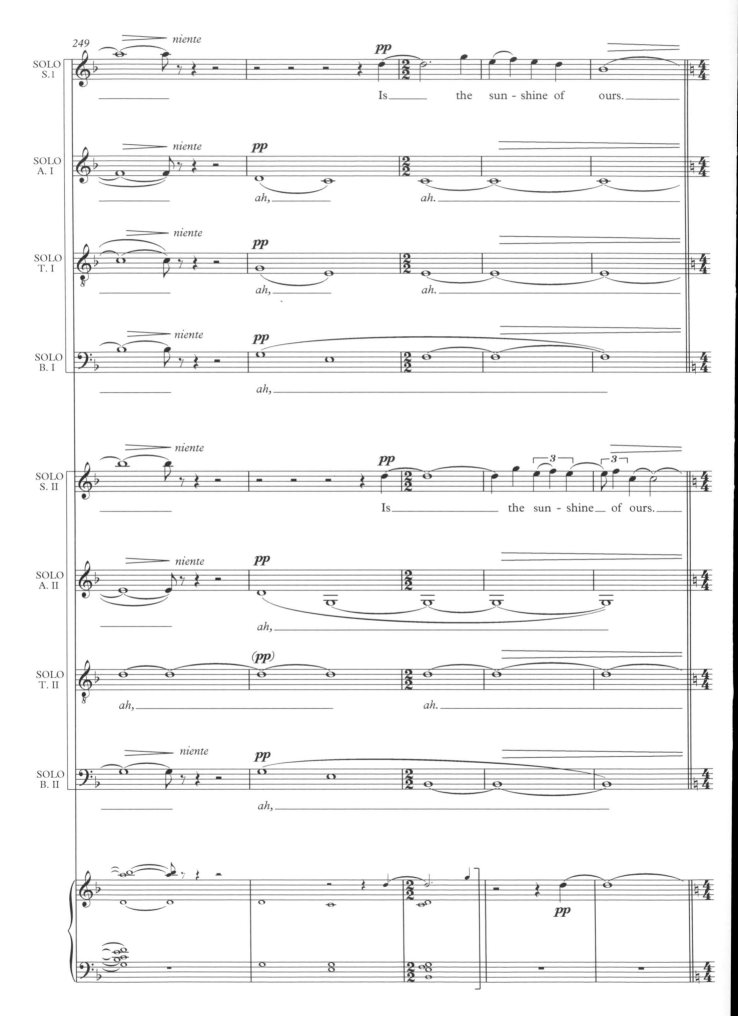

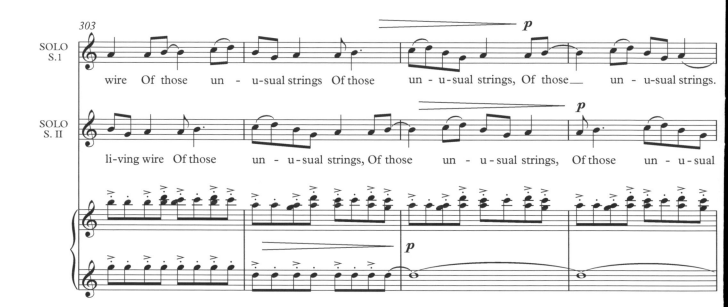

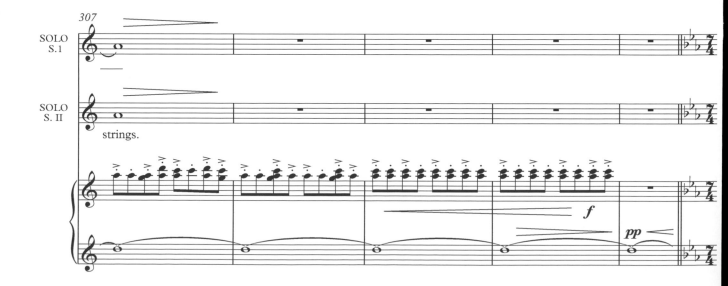

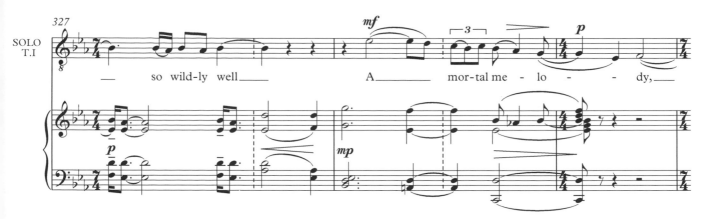

so wild-ly well___ A___ mor-tal me - lo - dy,___

A mor - tal me - lo - dy,___

A mor - tal me - lo - dy,___

A mor - tal me - lo - dy,___

Ah.___

* Stagger breathing as necessary.

73

* Stagger breathing as necessary.

Order no. NOV200508
ISBN 978-1-84772-777-0
Full score NOV200497-01
String quartet parts (set) NOV200497-01

© 2009 Novello & Company Ltd.

Published in Great Britain by
Novello Publishing Limited
(part of the Music Sales Group)

Head office: 14/15 Berners Street,
London W1T 3LJ, England
Tel. +44 (0)20 7612 7400
Fax +44 (0)20 7612 7545

Sales and Hire:
Music Sales Distribution Centre,
Newmarket Road, Bury St Edmunds,
Suffolk IP33 3YB
Tel. +44 (0)1284 702600
Fax +44 (0)1284 768301

www.chesternovello.com
e-mail: music@musicsales.co.uk

All Rights reserved

Printed in Great Britain

No part of this publication may be copied
or reproduced in any form or by any
means without the prior permission of
Novello & Company Limited.